THE JOY OF
EATING
RIGHT!

A BIBLE STUDY FOR WOMEN

THE JOY OF
EATING
RIGHT!

*Spiritual and Nutritional
Principles for Weight Control*

*Dee Brestin
and
Peggy Johnston*

VICTOR BOOKS

A DIVISION OF SCRIPTURE PRESS PUBLICATIONS INC.
USA CANADA ENGLAND

OTHER TITLES BY DEE BRESTIN

The Joy of Women's Friendships (Victor)
The Joy of Hospitality (Victor)
The Friendships of Women (Victor)
Accompanying Leader's Guide available
The Lifestyles of Christian Women (Victor)
Accompanying Leader's Guide available

Fisherman Bible studyguides (Harold Shaw Publishers)
Proverbs and Parables
Ecclesiastes
Examining the Claims of Christ (John 1–5)
1, 2 Peter and Jude
How Should a Christian Live? (1, 2, 3 John)
Higher Ground
Building Your House on the Lord: Marriage and Parenthood
Friendship: Portraits from God's Family Album

Most Scripture quotations are from the *Holy Bible, New International Version®*. Copyright © 1973, 1978, 1984 by International Bible Society. Used by permission of Zondervan Publishing House. All rights reserved; other Scriptures are taken from (AMP) *The Amplified New Testament* © 1954, 1958 The Lockman Foundation; (NASB) *New American Standard Bible*, © the Lockman Foundation 1960, 1962, 1963, 1968, 1971, 1972, 1973, 1975, 1977; (NKJV) *The New King James Version*. © 1979, 1980, 1982, Thomas Nelson, Inc., Publishers; (PH) J.B. Phillips: *The New Testament in Modern English*, Revised Edition, © J.B. Phillips, 1958, 1960, 1972, permission of Macmillan Publishing Co. and Collins Publishers.

Copyediting: Pamela T. Campbell
Cover Design: Joe DeLeon

Recommended Dewey Decimal Classification: 248.4
Suggested Subject Heading: CHRISTIAN LIVING

Library of Congress Catalog Card Number: 92-42311
ISBN: 0-89693-879-4

2   3   4   5   6   7   8   9   10   Printing/Year   97   96   95   94   93

VICTOR BOOKS
A division of SP Publications, Inc.
Wheaton, Illinois 60187

Contents

Introduction

You are about to embark on an adventure! This study is part of a series designed to help women live out significant Christianity in specific areas of their lives.

To some, developing healthy habits with food and exercise may not seem like a significant lifestyle issue. But those who have tested this guide will tell you differently. Here are some of their testimonies:

> I never realized before that my eating habits were related to my obedience to God. As I am developing obedience in this area of my life, it is radiating out to other areas of my walk.

> I've been to other diet groups, but none that dealt with the spiritual dimension, and I've come to realize that my poor eating habits are a spiritual problem. Another emphasis I've come to appreciate is that the habits I've learned during these 10 weeks are not a diet, but a lifestyle. I'm going through the guide again, right away, with a friend, to help cement those lifestyle habits.

> This guide spills over into all of life: topics like perspective, persistence, and convictions have a much broader application than just my eating habits.

> I've never been through a study that kept me so accountable! There were times when I considered bailing out, but I'm so thankful I didn't—not only because of the weight I lost, but because I've seen some real changes in my eating habits.

It's common for weight control support groups to begin with many members and then dwindle. Therefore, make a commitment now to yourself and to the other group members, to stay with the group for the entire study, to weigh in every week, and to do the disciplines required. Sometimes it will be painful, but there's seldom victory without a cost. Determine now to pay the cost.

BEFORE YOU BEGIN

Because of the nature of this guide, the chapters are divided into daily assignments, as victory will be accomplished only by daily diligence. When your Food Journal pages in the Appendix are filled, buy an extra notebook to record your food plan and your actual intake. In the Appendix you'll also find a Habit Graph, sample recipes, a Weight Graph, and a list of additional recommended reading materials. These are all important tools to help you find victory and joy in eating right!

For best results, we recommend you do this study in a group, or with at least one other person to whom you will be accountable.

If you are leading this group, you will find helps for each chapter in the back of this guide. When you complete this guide, suggestions for follow-up are at the end of the last session.

One
Support Groups

ACCOUNTABILITY TIME

Weigh in. Your discussion leader or partner will weigh you and keep your weight confidential. Record your starting weight on the Weight Graph in the Appendix. (This graph does not show your actual weight, though you may record it if you prefer.) It's a good idea to also record your measurements now. (When you aren't losing pounds, check and see if you are losing inches.)

Beginning next week, this Accountability Time will include breaking into groups of two or three to:
A. Share the memory verse designed to help you fight temptation.
B. Share your Weight Graph, Habit Graph, and Food Journal.

WARMUP

Get ready to introduce yourself to the group. Share your name, a little about yourself, and why you are here. (For example, "I'm Peggy Johnston. I have a husband and two small boys who are both a delight and a challenge to me, and I teach a weekly children's Bible club. I'm glad to be here to have a chance to be with women and to have the group accountability for my eating habits!")

SPIRITUAL PRINCIPLE

As believers with a common concern, we can be a great help to each other through accountability, encouragement, and prayer.

The Joy of Eating Right!

Read Ecclesiastes 4:9-12.

1. Does this passage provide any basis for having a support group? Explain.

2. Have you found help from support groups to strengthen positive areas of your life? (Bible study, or prayer, or eating habits, or other lifestyle issues?) If so, share why you did better with a support group than you did alone.

3. "Three strands" (v. 12) could be applied to bringing God into a friendship. What are some ways we could tap into the power of God in this support group?

Read Hebrews 3:12-13.

4. How often, according to this passage, should we be encouraging one another? *daily* Why? Though we are only meeting weekly, what are some ways we could encourage one another daily? *It's so easy to become "hardened" by sin's deceitfulness, that I've daily got to stay on top of it!*

5. Can you think of examples of how you have deceived yourself about eating habits? How could keeping a Food Journal and Habit Graph change that? *What's this one sweet roll going to do to me today? I'll start dieting tomorrow — what's one more day?*

Read Hebrews 10:23-25.

6. What is "the hope we profess"? *Hope in Christ, the hope of better things to come —*

7. Why, according to verse 23, can we be confident of victory in overcoming sinful habits? Is there an area of your life where you have seen positive change because of your trust in Christ? (Sometimes it's difficult to share this without seeming proud, but remember you are sharing what you have seen Christ do in you, and this will be an encouragement to the group.)

8. According to verses 24-25, how can we increase the effective- ness of group support? *— meeting together, encouraging each other.*

Comment on the following reflection:

> Beginning next week, we will help each other overcome sin's deceitfulness by pairing off and listening to each other's memory work and looking at each other's Food Journals, and Weight and Habit Graphs. The way that we approach this will impact our effectiveness. Sometimes women, who may be tender and empathic, will not look carefully at a friend's Food Journal or Habit Graph, for fear of embarrassing her. Or, if a friend confesses that she has been disobedient or hasn't learned her verse, a woman may make the mistake of sympathizing with her sin. This approach, instead of "helping her up," actually keeps her down. A more helpful approach might be to say something like: "Why do you think you fail? How can I pray for you?" Then pray for her!

Read Galatians 6:1-5.
9. How, according to verse 1, are we to treat a sister overtaken by a sin? *— Restore gently but watch ourselves — carry each others burdens*

11

This passage deals primarily with the burden of overcoming sin, though it could apply to other kinds of burdens. In verse 1, the word *restore* is used in secular Greek for setting broken bones. In verse 2, the word translated *burdens* means an overburden.

10. Imagine that a friend has had a terrible week (an "overburden") with her eating habits. Describe how you might gently restore her.

In verse 5, the word translated *load* means a "normal, everyday load."

11. What is your responsibility in carrying your everyday load concerning finding victory with your eating habits? *To take one everyday load at a time and be responsible for it myself —*

Meditate on James 5:16.

12. What principles for effective group prayer do you find in James 5:16?

NUTRITION PRINCIPLE

Look over the Appendix together. You'll be choosing one of the diet plans, keeping a Food Journal, and daily charting your eating habits on the Habit Graph.

PRAYER TIME

Though Jesus talked about the power of "two agreeing in prayer" (Matthew 18:19), many people are frightened at the thought of praying out loud in a group. However, we think you'll find "Popcorn Prayer" unintimidating.

"Popcorn Prayer" means that the leader lifts up a woman's name.

Then two or three or four say *a sentence prayer* about that woman and everyone else prays silently. Then, when the "popping" stops, the leader introduces another woman. You don't know where the prayers are going to come from, just as you don't know which popcorn kernels are going to pop.

Today you might want to introduce the women's names one by one for Popcorn Prayer, asking God to help them get off to a good start in overcoming their bad eating habits. Here's a sample prayer time:

Leader: Lord, we lift up Linda to You.

Sue: Father, please give Linda wisdom in choosing one of the food programs in the Appendix.

Lori: I agree, Lord.

Anne: Please help Linda to be faithful in planning her food choices and recording them.

Lori: And please help her in using the memory verse when she's tempted.

Sue: I agree, Lord.

Leader: Father, we lift up Sue to You.

NEXT WEEK'S ASSIGNMENT
1. Choose a weight control program for the following week from one of the choices in the Appendix today.
2. Plan your food choices for tomorrow, either in the Appendix or in a separate notebook. Record any deviations. (See the model Food Journal in the Appendix.)
3. Do the daily assignments in Chapter 2. It begins tomorrow!
4. Daily record your success on your Habit Graph. (See Appendix.)

Two

Perspective

ACCOUNTABILITY TIME
Weigh in. Record your progress on the graph in the Appendix.

As you wait to weigh in, or as you assemble afterward, share with a partner or small group:
A. Your memory verse (Hebrews 12:11).
B. Your Weight Graph, Habit Graph, and Food Journal.

WARMUP
Stressed, spelled backward, is desserts! Unfortunately, that's the way many of us have trained ourselves to react to stress (or boredom, or loneliness, or pain). Each woman should share here name and a stressful situation she either faced last week or faces frequently. (For example, "I am Dee Brestin and I received a letter today from a woman who was angry about something I wrote in one of my books. I considered reaching for chips!")

After everyone has shared, ask: **How do you feel after you have tried to use food to meet a spiritual need?**

SPIRITUAL PRINCIPLE
We must see food as God does. He created it to meet the needs of the body, not the soul. When we reach for food to ease pain, rather than hunger, we are reinforcing harmful habit patterns. We must

retrain ourselves to eat only when we are hungry.

DAY 1
. . . .
Choose your food plan from one in the Appendix. Write down what you plan to eat today in a notebook. Keep your plan nearby and scrupulously record any additions or changes.

Memorize Hebrews 12:11.

> No discipline seems pleasant at the time, but painful. Later on, however, it produces a harvest of righteousness and peace for those who have been trained by it.

Hint: Memorize a word at a time. "No . . . No discipline . . . No discipline seems," etc.

Read Hebrews 12:11-13.
1. What do you learn about discipline from these verses?

Most people who struggle with eating right have "lame limbs." They have developed the habit of thinking of food as a way to alleviate stress or pain. They need to retrain themselves to see food as a way to nourish the body, not the soul. In his helpful book, *Diets Still Don't Work* (Breakthru Publishing, 1990), Bob Schwartz describes the way thin people think and eat:

1. They don't eat unless their body is HUNGRY.
2. They don't eat unconsciously; they ENJOY every bite of what they are eating and they are aware of the effect the food is having on their bodies.
3. They stop eating when their bodies are no longer hungry.
4. They eat EXACTLY what they want—EXACTLY what will satisfy them.

We would qualify the above from a Christian perspective. It is true that many thin people survive on junk food. However, God intended food to nourish the body, so we must also train ourselves to like the four food groups and to LIMIT OUR FAT. We can learn, however, from this principle, to plan some foods in our day that we really enjoy, in moderation, so that we don't feel deprived.

2. Without looking at the above list, describe the way thin people eat. How is this different from the way you eat?

DAY 2 . . . .
Record your food plan. Mark your Habit Graph. Finish memorizing Hebrews 12:11.

Meditate on Hebrews 12:11.
3. Have you accepted that there is going to be pain involved in changing your eating habits? What is most painful to you?

Meditate on Hebrews 12:13.
4. Why, according to this verse, must you change your responses to food? Remembering how thin people think, describe some level paths for your feet.

DAY 3 . . . .
Record your food plan. Mark your Habit Graph. Review and use Hebrews 12:11.

Read Genesis 25:24-35.
5. When Esau came in from the open country, what was uppermost in his mind?

6. The birthright not only guaranteed the firstborn a spiritual blessing, but also provided him with a double portion of the inheritance, the best land, and the honor of the position. With the value of the birthright in mind, what kind of value had Esau placed on the food in front of him?

7. How do you value the pleasure of eating in comparison to the value of being healthy, thin, and more disciplined? Write down some of the joys you anticipate when you are closer to your long-term goal.

DAY 4
Record your food plan. Mark your Habit Graph. Review your memory verse.

8. What might have been Esau's perspective at the time he made the decision to sell his birthright in Genesis 25?

9. What is your perspective when you choose to eat food you don't need? Write down your thoughts so that you'll better be able to recognize their deceptiveness next time.

10. Are there other areas of your life (integrity in areas of money, sex, power; laziness in relationships with people or God; etc.) in which you may be making long-term compromises for the temporary satisfaction of today?

Dee's Reflection

We live in a world of instant potatoes, microwave ovens, easy credit, and quick divorce. But weight control is a long-term project. It may take months or even years of perseverance to achieve healthy eating habits and a lean body.

DAY 5
. . . .
Record your food plan. Mark your Habit Graph. Review your memory verse.

Read Philippians 3:12-14.
11. In Paul's spiritual pilgrimage, what did he acknowledge which might be useful to you in your weight control journey?

Peg's Reflection

In leading weight control programs at our local college, I've seen that a history of failure can be an obstacle to success. Many people begin weight control programs thinking: *I've never been successful before, but maybe there will be something different this time. I guess it's worth a try.* They don't truly commit themselves, and they don't really have any goal in mind. It's just another halfhearted attempt destined for failure.

12. Paul mentions the need to forget about what is behind us and press on toward the prize. What is your prize? What is your goal? Is it attainable? Is it realistic? Are you truly committed, no matter how long it takes? Take some time to think about these questions and record your thoughts below.

In *Strengthening Your Grip* (Word, 1990) Chuck Swindoll wrote "Attitude alone fuels my fire or assaults my hope. When my attitudes are right there's no barrier too high, no valley too deep, no dream too extreme, and no challenge too great for me."

DAYS 6 AND 7

Record your food plan. Mark your Habit Graph. Review your memory verse. Read and complete the nutrition section.

NUTRITION PRINCIPLE

Understanding meal planning. It's foolish to go into battle without a game plan. Plan your meals and snacks a day at a time. If you find you need to revise your plan during the day, write down what and how much you will eat **before** you deviate.

Choose wisely for a well-balanced diet. No matter what diet plan you are following, include the four basic food groups. An adult needs a variety of foods in the following quantities:

 2 servings — Milk and Dairy
 2 servings — Meat and Substitutes
 4 servings — Breads and Cereals
 4 servings — Fruits and Vegetables

If you choose low fat, low sugar foods from these groups, you will get approximately 1,200 calories each day, which is an appropriate calorie level for almost any woman to lose weight. If a woman cannot lose weight on 1,200 calories, it is wise to increase the amount of calories expended in activity or to cut back further on fat rather than to cut back on calories consumed.

Use variety and try to include at least three food groups at each meal.

True/False Test #1

1. T F   Meal planning must be done at the beginning of the week for a whole week at a time.
2. T F   If you find you need to deviate, record what and how much you will eat before you revise your plan.
3. T F   Meal plans of 1,200 calories per day provide an adequate weight loss program for most women.

(See Appendix for answers.)

Application

This week I am going to apply the following lesson from this chapter:

This week, when I plan my meals, I am going to:

Three

The Joy of Obedience

ACCOUNTABILITY TIME
Weigh in. Record your progress on the graph in the Appendix.

As you are waiting to weigh in, or as you assemble afterward, share with a partner or small group:
A. Your memory verse (Genesis 4:6-7a).
B. Your Weight Graph, Habit Graph, and Food Journal.

WARMUP
Have women share some victories (eating habits, weight loss, Food Journal, etc.)! Then ask them to share their feelings.

SPIRITUAL PRINCIPLE
Joy springs from obedience. Disobedience never leads to lasting joy.

DAY 1 . . . .
Record your food plan. In addition, this week, at the end of each day, record how you feel about your day's eating habits. Record your Habit Graph.

Begin memorizing the following verse:

Then the Lord said to Cain, "Why are you angry? And why

has your countenance fallen? If you do well, will not your countenance be lifted up?" (Genesis 4:6-7a, NASB)

Next week you will finish this important passage.

DAY 2
Record your food plan, your feelings about your day's eating habits, and your Habit Graph. Finish memorizing Genesis 4:6-7a.

Read Romans 12:1-2.
1. What does Paul plead with us to do in verses 1-2? Why?

2. How could you apply this passage to your eating habits?

3. The "pattern of this world" in regard to food is to use it to satisfy the soul. In regard to body shape, it is to be as thin as a model. How do you think God would have you transform your thinking concerning these two "world patterns"? Be specific.

4. What significance do you see in the fact that this is a "living" sacrifice rather than a once and for all sacrifice?

Jerry Bridges, in *The Pursuit of Holiness* (NavPress, 1978), writes:

True holiness includes control over our physical bodies and appetites. . . . Quite possibly there is no greater conformity to the world among evangelical Christians today than the way in which we, instead of presenting our bodies as holy sacrifices, pamper and indulge them in defiance of our better judgment and our Christian purpose in life.

DAY 3
· ·
Record your food plan, your feelings, your Habit Graph. Review the memory verse.

5. The word *sacrifice* may make you feel like this is not going to be much fun. Put Romans 12:1 together with the following words of Jesus and see if you can state a more positive view of the command to "offer your body as a living sacrifice."

   If you obey My commands, you will remain in My love, just as I have obeyed My Father's commands and remain in His love. I have told you this so that My joy may be in you and that your joy may be complete (John 15:10-11).

Cain did not offer a sacrifice that was pleasing to God, and the result was depression. Then the Lord said to Cain:

   "Why are you angry? And why has your countenance fallen? If you do well, will not your countenance be lifted up? And if you do not do well, sin is crouching at the door; and its desire is for you, but you must master it" (Genesis 4:6-7).

6. According to the above passage, what were Cain's two options? What were the corresponding consequences?

DAY 4
· ·
Record Food Journal, feelings, and Habit Graph. Review memory verse.

7. Can you identify with the Lord's words to Cain in your memory verse? Have you experienced depression as a result of eating habits that are not holy and pleasing to God? Conversely, have

you experienced joy as a result of self-control? Share something about your feelings in each situation.

8. When you have chosen disobedience, have you experienced the tentacles of sin which grasped Cain? Share something about it.

Counselor Jay Adams says, in *Competent to Counsel* (Presbyterian and Reformed Pub. Co., 1978) that the relationship between feelings and behavior is set forth very clearly in Scripture. For example, Peter often pointed out that good living produces good feelings and that good deeds (in the full biblical sense of the term) lead to good days (see Psalm 34:12-13).

DAY 5 ....
Spend this quiet time in prayer and reflection.

9. Before you record your food plan today, pray about it. Ask God to give you wisdom in planning. What is He impressing on your heart?

10. Read over the feelings you recorded in your Food Journal. What did you learn about yourself?

11. Record your Habit Graph. Examine it prayerfully. Do you see any pattern that teaches you something about yourself?

Pray through the verses in this lesson, asking God to use them to transform your mind. Review your memory verse, asking God to bring it to your remembrance throughout the day — whenever you are tempted to choose the course that will make you downcast.

Remember: NOTHING TASTES AS GREAT AS BEING THIN FEELS!

DAYS 6 AND 7
Record food, Habit Graph, and review your memory verse! Read and complete the nutrition section.

NUTRITION PRINCIPLE
Understanding body and dietary fat. Any weight control effort needs to focus on a healthy body fat level, not just weight loss. If possible, have your body fat percentage determined, either by hydrostatic weighing, impedance, or skin fold tests. Possible places this could be done in your community are: health clubs, a wellness oriented medical clinic, or the exercise physiology department at a local college or university. This will give you a more realistic weight goal than will a height-weight chart.

Fat is the most concentrated source of calories, and fat calories are converted into body fat more readily than carbohydrate or protein calories. Recent research shows that women can eat more calories yet lose more weight when fat intake is limited to 20% of calorie intake. (The average American eats 42% of his/her calories from fat.) Put a check mark (√) next to the high fat items that are included in your diet almost daily. Put an asterisk next to those that you eat almost weekly.

___ snack crackers	___ chips	___ fried foods
___ butter, margarine	___ pastries	___ cream soups
___ fatty meats	___ cookies	___ ice cream
___ luncheon meats	___ cheese	___ nuts, seeds
___ creamy sauces	___ hot dogs	___ whole milk
___ peanut butter	___ granola	___ mayonnaise
___ donuts, rolls	___ desserts	___ salad dressings

Reducing fat not only helps in weight control, but is important for a healthy heart and may reduce the risk of developing some types of cancer.

True/False Test #2

1. T F A height-weight chart is the best resource for a realistic weight goal.

2. T F A calorie is a calorie! 2 grams of fat is the same as 2 grams of carbohydrate or protein.

3. T F If I eat less fat, I can eat more food for less calories.

(See Appendix for answers.)

Application

This week I am asking God to help me be obedient in the following way:

This week I am going to concentrate on lowering my intake of fat by:

Four

Self-Control

ACCOUNTABILITY TIME

Weigh in. Record your progress on the graph in the Appendix.

Reassemble. Today, you will be sharing your memory work of Genesis 4:6-7, Habit Graph, Food Journal or, if you choose, your Weight Graph with the whole group.

WARMUP

Ask: **What value do wedding vows have?** You might consider how a person's fear of God impacts her values, how values strengthen a person to resist temptation, etc.

SPIRITUAL PRINCIPLE

God has provided His children with the power to control the flesh and to live by His Spirit.

DAY 1 . . . .

Record your food plan.

Finish memorizing this passage:

> Then the Lord said to Cain, "Why are you angry? And why has your countenance fallen? If you do well, will not your countenance be lifted up? And if you do not do well, sin is

crouching at the door; and its desire is for you, but you must master it" (Genesis 4:6-7, NASB).

DAY 2 . . . .
Record your food plan and your Habit Graph. Review Genesis 4:6-7.

1. When God said to Cain, "You must master it," what was He implying about our ability to overcome sin?

On *Focus on the Family* (11/29/92) Dr. James Dobson, in talking about eating right, said he told an overweight friend: "There's only one answer. You need to get on your face before God and promise you will never eat that way again."

Dee's Reflection
I am strengthened by making promises to God. However, I prefer to make daily promises and to promise that "Today, I will eat the way a person with good eating habits eats." I have also memorized Ecclesiastes 5:1-7 to help me keep my promise.

Read Ecclesiastes 5:1-7.
2. What are some reasons, according to this passage, that we should keep the vows we make to God?

Read Romans 7:14-25.
3. Describe Paul's battle. Describe the battle that goes on in you with regard to weight control.

In his article, "The Sin of Self Discipline," (*Discipleship Journal*, March 1, 1988, issue 44) psychologist Larry Crabb says that self-control is better than self-discipline because it goes deeper. He explains that a person exercising self-discipline thinks: *This is something I should not do. Therefore, I will not do it.* The person exercising self-control, however, goes a step further. He thinks: *I really don't want to even though there is a part of me that does. But the deepest part of me that understands where real life is found does not want to do this, and therefore I'm honoring who I really am in Christ by walking away from it.* The difference between *should* and *want to* is a profound secret.

4. Imagine the following scenario. Your neighbor has delivered a plate of chocolate chip cookies for your family. The plate is sitting on the counter, calling to you. You are not hungry, but you are bored.
   A. What would be a natural response?

   B. What would be a reflective response? (Ask yourself, Who am I? What do I really want?)

DAY 3

Reflect on your Habit Graph and Food Journal. Spend some time in confession. Plan today's food choices, remembering to bring healthy variety into your menu.

Review Genesis 4:6-7. Use it today!

Read Romans 8:1-16.

5. Take some time to discover the secrets of tapping into the power of the Holy Spirit in the following verses:

   vv. 1-4:

   vv. 5-8:

Jerry Bridges says, in *The Practice of Godliness* (NavPress, 1983):

> Our minds are mental green houses, where unlawful thoughts, once planted, are nurtured and watered before being transplanted into the real world of unlawful actions. People seldom fall suddenly into gluttony or immorality. These actions are savored in the mind long before they are enjoyed in reality. The thought life, then, is our first line of defense in the battle of self-control.

vv. 13-14

DAY 4 ....

Read Galatians 5:13-16.
6. With privilege comes responsibility. What privilege and what responsibility does Paul mention in verse 13? How could you apply this to a weight control program?

The Amplified Bible translates verse 16 as follows: "But I say, walk *and* live habitually in the (Holy) Spirit—responsive to *and* controlled *and* guided by the Spirit; then you will certainly not gratify the cravings *and* desires of the flesh—of human nature without God" (AMP).

7. Is the Habit Graph and Food Journal helping you to learn to walk habitually by the Holy Spirit in response to food choices? How could this tool be more effective in your life?

Mark your Habit Graph thoughtfully. Prayerfully plan your food choices for today.

DAY 5 . . . .

Read Galatians 5:17-26.

8. List some of the contrasting acts of each of the following.

The Sinful Nature   **The Spirit**

9. Now apply this to your battle with weight control. Using your imagination, list some of the contrasting acts of each of the following in your struggle with weight control.

The Sinful Nature   **The Spirit**

I'm too lazy to plan my day's   I prayerfully plan my day's
food choices.   food choices.

"Like a city whose walls are broken down is a man who lacks self-control" (Proverbs 25:28).

DAYS 6 AND 7 . . . .

Keep up with your Habit Graph and Food Journal. Review Genesis 4:6-7 and apply it! Read and complete the nutrition section.

NUTRITION PRINCIPLE

Understanding Carbohydrates. Low carbohydrate diets were popular several years ago and people lost weight on them, but most of the weight loss was from water, not body fat. Furthermore, while on these diets, people harmed their bodies by overloading on saturated fats and cholesterol. Complex carbohydrates are our friends — not our enemies. God designed complex carbohydrates to be the major source of fuel for the body. Studies show that people

31

who choose complex carbohydrates for 50-60% of their calories are going to be more successful in lifetime weight control. Carbohydrates come in simple forms, called sugars; more complex forms, called starch; and very complex forms, called fiber.

Most of us would do well to increase the amount of complex carbohydrates and decrease our simple carbohydrates (sugars). If we select well, we can get large amounts of vitamins and minerals from complex carbohydrates with only trace amounts of fat.

Look over your food plan. How many servings of each of the following do you have planned for today?

___ fresh fruits, or fruits canned without sugar
___ fresh vegetables, or those processed without salt
___ whole grain bread and crackers
___ whole grain cereals, unsweetened
___ pasta

Americans could improve their diets by cutting sugar intake and increasing starch and fiber intake. Sugar is high in calories, low in nutrients, and low in filling power! Consider these concentrated sources of sugar. Put a check mark (√) by those that you have eaten in the last three days.

___ sugar	___ soft drinks	___ pastries
___ honey	___ gelatin	___ candy
___ jam	___ puddings	___ cookies
___ jelly	___ sweetened fruit	___ cake
___ marmalade	___ sugarcoated cereal	___ doughnuts
___ pies	___ sweet rolls	___ frozen treats
___ molasses	___ corn syrup	___ maple syrup

True/False Test #3

1. T F Low-carbohydrate diets are a good way to lose weight.

2. T F Simple carbohydrates are sugar, complex are starch, and very complex are fiber.

3. T F Choosing complex carbohydrates for 50-60% of your diet will help you to develop and maintain a healthy body.

(See Appendix for answers.)

Application

This week I am going to apply the following lesson from this chapter:

This week at the grocery store, I am going to buy more of the following complex carbohydrates:

Five

The Heart

ACCOUNTABILITY TIME
Weigh in. Record your progress on the graph in the Appendix.

As you are waiting to weigh in, or as you assemble afterward, share with a partner or your small group your Weight Graph, Habit Graph, and Food Journal. Without giving excuses, talk about some of the areas where you are struggling. Pray in twos briefly.

WARMUP
The following exercise is sure to warm your hearts! If your group is large, you may want to divide so that it doesn't cut into your discussion time. Go around the room, and take turns commenting on strengths you see in the women present. At most, four comments. Then move to the next woman. For example:

Eileen: I have appreciated Brenda's enthusiasm in this group. Sometimes I've come discouraged, but Brenda's encouragement and hope always lift me.

Ila: I've noticed how thoroughly you do the lessons, Brenda — and that's been a good example to me.

Karla: Brenda's a very sensitive person. She listens carefully and can remember something someone said three weeks ago!

SPIRITUAL PRINCIPLE

Basic to change is the heart. First, we need to allow God to cleanse our hearts in salvation. Then we need to keep our hearts cleansed by repenting when we are aware of sin and asking God to renew a steadfast spirit within us.

DAY 1
Record your food plan. (Remember to plan variety!) Record your Habit Graph.

Memorize Psalm 51:10.

Create in me a clean heart, O God, and renew a steadfast spirit within me.

DAY 2
Record your food plan and Habit Graph.

Read Matthew 15:1-2, 10-20.
1. The "religious men" were concerned about being unclean because of ceremonially "unclean" hands. What does Jesus teach makes a man unclean? Why?

Read Matthew 13:1-9, 18-23.
2. What three things prevent a fruitful harvest as the message of Christ's kingdom is sown? Comment on how you would apply each of these things to two aspects of your life: first, your relationship to Christ; and second, your weight control program.

A. v. 19

35

B. v. 21

C. v. 22

DAY 3 ....

Record your food plan and Habit Graph.

Read 1 Timothy 4:8.
3. What is of more value than weight control training? Why?

The central message of the Bible has to do with the cleansing of our hearts so that we may be reconciled with God and be with Him in heaven when we die. All of us are in need of cleansing. Solomon says: "Who can say, 'I have kept my heart pure; I am clean and without sin'?" (Proverbs 20:9)

Read 1 Peter 2:24-25.
4. Explain God's plan for cleansing you, if you choose to trust in it.

DAY 4 ....

Record your food plan and Habit Graph.

Isaiah 1:18b says: "Though your sins are like scarlet, they shall be as white as snow." If you have trusted Christ for your salvation, tell the group, in six sentences or less, how it happened and how His cleansing has changed you. There are two common kinds of conversions: a Paul Conversion (Paul was converted as an adult, out of a life of rebellion) and a Timothy Conversion (Timothy was converted as a little child). Choose the one that is closest to your story.

A. Paul Conversion
  1. Describe, in two sentences or less, what your life was like before you knew Christ:

  2. Describe, in two sentences or less, how the plan of salvation (that Christ died to pay for your sins) was explained to you and how you responded.

  3. Describe, in two sentences or less, how your life has changed because of Christ.

B. Timothy Conversion
  1. Describe, in three sentences or less, how the plan of salvation (that Christ died to pay for your sins) was explained to you as a little child and how you responded.

  2. Describe, in three sentences or less, how your life would be different if you hadn't known Christ.

DAY 5 . . . .
Record your food plan and Habit Graph.

Meditate on Psalm 51:10.
5. What insights does the Lord give you for personal application?

Read 1 John 1:5-9.

6. Explain what we must do the minute we are aware we've walked out of the light. Why?

7. Why is it vital to apply the above truth to your weight control program?

DAYS 6 AND 7 ....

Keep your Habit Graph. Read this section and then make your food plan.

NUTRITION PRINCIPLE

Understanding calorie balance. One pound of body fat stores approximately 3,500 calories. Diuretics, laxatives, and some fad diets will give only a temporary water loss. To lose a pound of body fat, reduce your caloric intake by 3,500 calories, or increase your caloric output by 3,500 calories.

To lose 10 pounds, you need to create a calorie deficit of 35,000 calories. To lose 10 pounds in a month, you'd need to cut back intake or increase output by 1,129 calories each day. To lose it in two months, you'd need to create a calorie deficit of about 565 calories each day. But if you set a goal to lose 10 pounds over the next year, you'd only have to average a calorie deficit of about 96 calories a day.

If you've tried to lose weight quickly in the past ("30 pounds by Christmas," "15 pounds by the reunion") and you are as heavy, or heavier than when you started those programs, maybe it is time to reevaluate your weight control mentality. If you lose 10 (maybe even 20) pounds a year for the next several years (if necessary), you're more apt to get and stay at your goal!

8. If a woman burns 2,000 calories a day, and is willing to eat 1,500 calories, how long will it take him to lose 10 pounds of body fat?

(See Appendix for answer.)

Application

This week I am going to apply the following lesson from this chapter:

Pray about how much you think God would have you weigh. Then, through prayer and planning, set some intermediate and long-term goals, with reasonable dates for achieving them.

Exchange Secret Sisters

Every woman who wishes to participate should put her name in a hat. Then pass the hat so that each woman can draw a secret sister. She will pray for her, send her encouraging notes, and perhaps small gifts. In five weeks, you'll reveal your secret sisters.

Six
Appetite and Hunger

ACCOUNTABILITY TIME
Weigh in. Record your progress on the graph in the Appendix.

As you are waiting to weigh in, or as you assemble afterward, share with a partner or your small group:
A. Your memory verse (Ephesians 4:27).
B. Your Weight Graph, Habit Graph, and Food Journal.

WARMUP
Our bodies can "hunger" for food, sex, sleep, clothing, shelter, and cleanliness. Hunger is a genuine God-given signal. Appetite, on the other hand, may be deceitful, telling us that more will satisfy us. I've learned to respond to my body's hunger for sleep at night. I go to bed when I'm tired, even if it's 9 P.M. or I'm in the middle of a good book. I've also learned to get up when I wake up, even if it's 5 A.M. because my hunger has been met, though my appetite for sleep could keep me in bed two more hours.

Take one of the above categories and make a contrast between hunger and appetite. What do you learn?

SPIRITUAL PRINCIPLE

The ability to distinguish between hunger and appetite is essential for a successful weight control program.

DAY 1

Record your food plan. Record your Habit Graph.

Memorize the following verse:

"Do not give the devil a foothold" (Ephesians 4:27).

1. What are ways you have given the devil a foothold in your weight control program?

2. What are ways you can obey this verse in your weight control program?

DAY 2

Read Ecclesiastes 10:16-17.

3. What things will bring woe onto a land? And what things will bring blessing? Why do you suppose this is true?

4. How can you relate the phrase "eat at a proper time—for strength and not for drunkenness" to your personal eating habits?

Make your food plan for the day, writing down approximate times for eating as well as what you will eat. Mark your Habit Graph.

DAY 3
. . . .

Make your food plan for the day. If it was helpful to plan times for eating as well, do that again. Mark your Habit Graph.

Read Ecclesiastes 6:7-9.

5. What are the implications of the statement that Solomon makes in verse 7?

6. Describe what a "roving appetite" is like in your life. According to verse 9, what is its result? Can you identify with this? Explain.

7. How might you prevent the devil from getting a foothold with your roving appetite?

DAY 4
. . . .

Make your food plan. Mark your Habit Graph.

Read Proverbs 25:16.

8. What does this verse tell you about the difference between hunger and appetite? What are some ways you can discern the difference in yourself?

Read Philippians 3:17-21.
9. List all the characteristics you can discover about those who are bent on satisfying their appetites.

10. List all you can discover about those whose citizenship is in heaven.

DAY 5 ....
Make your food plan. Mark your Habit Graph.

Read 1 John 2:15-17.
11. How do these verses provide perspective on indulging our appetites?

Research shows that overweight people are much more likely to eat in response to external cues (appetite), and normal weight people are more likely to eat in response to internal cues (hunger). Appetite is stimulated by the sight and smell of food, the availability of food, the time of day, and social input.

12. How could you limit external cues in your life in order to decrease temptation?

Whenever you are desiring to eat, ask yourself if it is hunger or appetite. If you can't tell, get involved in another activity. If in 20 minutes the desire is still there, satisfy it with a lower calorie snack. The more you feed your appetites the more they grow and master you.

Work on minimizing food cues in your kitchen by reorganizing and throwing out. Pray through Psalm 141:3 first. Then do this reorganizing with a friend, or during a time of day when you are strong.

13. Give a brief report on what you did to minimize food cues in your kitchen.

DAYS 6 AND 7
. . . .
Record your food plan and Habit Graph. Read and complete the nutrition section.

NUTRITION PRINCIPLE
Supermarket strategy. Plan ahead. Don't go into the battle without a game plan! Below are some tips to apply every time you shop:

1. Have a menu plan.

2. Limit the portion size of high calorie or high cost items. If you prepare a meal for five, but have enough casserole to feed eight, you're likely to eat it all, when your family could have filled up on low fat vegetables, rice, and fruit instead.

3. Have a shopping list. This minimizes last-minute decisions and impulse buying. To make your list:
   A. Keep a running list of items you're low on.
   B. Check the grocery ads to plan or revise your menu.
   C. Make the remainder of your list from your menu plan.

4. In the supermarket, do not vary from your list, or you may very well be giving the devil a foothold. Do not respond to visual cues and buy on impulse. Be aware of grocery marketing techniques such as placing impulse items like chips, soda pop, and holiday candies at the end aisles.

5. Don't shop when you are hungry.

Reading Labels. Take the time to read nutrition labels, so that you can make the best possible selection for your food dollar.

Application
This week I am going to apply the following lesson from this chapter:

This week, before going grocery shopping, I am going to:

Seven
Overcoming Temptation

ACCOUNTABILITY TIME
Weigh in. Record your progress on the graph in the Appendix.

As you are waiting to weigh in, or as you assemble afterward, share with a partner or small group:
A. Your memory verse (Hebrews 4:15-16).
B. Your Weight Graph, Habit Graph, and Food Journal.

WARMUP
Can you think of a time when you turned from a temptation (something you considered watching, doing, or saying) because of a Scripture or scriptural principle that came to mind? Share it with the group.

SPIRITUAL PRINCIPLE
Jesus was tempted in His life on earth, but He never sinned by giving in to temptation. We can learn to overcome temptation as Jesus did.

DAY 1
If you would like to choose a different diet plan from the Appendix for this week, do so. Record your food plan and Habit Graph.

Begin memorizing Hebrews 4:15-16.

For we do not have a high priest who is unable to sympathize with our weaknesses, but we have one who has been tempted in every way, just as we are — yet was without sin. Let us then approach the throne of grace with confidence, so that we may receive mercy and find grace to help us in our time of need.

1. How might you apply Hebrews 4:15-16 today?

DAY 2 . . . .
Record your food plan, remembering to revise if you plan to deviate. Don't eat any unplanned food. Record your Habit Graph.

Finish memorizing Hebrews 4:15-16.

Read Matthew 4:1-4.
2. Describe the scene, Satan's temptation, and the method through which Jesus overcame it.

3. What might the future consequences have been if Jesus had not overcome Satan's temptations?

4. The following are common temptations which we face in the area of weight control. Consider the consequences of obedience/ disobedience in each area. Try to find a Scripture which would strengthen you to overcome each temptation, either from past memory verses or other verses.

   A. You are attracted to a special holiday candy display in the grocery store, and are considering deviating from your list.

Consequences of obedience/disobedience?

Scripture to help you overcome this temptation?

B. You are stressed and feeling that chocolate cake might help.

Consequences of obedience/disobedience?

Scripture to help you overcome this temptation?

C. You're forced to change your lunch menu and don't want to take the time to write down your planned deviation.

Consequences of obedience/disobedience?

Scripture to help you overcome this temptation?

D. Describe a frequent temptation for you (snacking, desserts, seconds).

Consequences of obedience/disobedience?

Scripture to help you overcome this temptation?

DAY 3 . . . .
Record your Food Journal and Habit Graph.

Read 2 Timothy 3:1-5.
5. What are some of the characteristics of the person who is a

lover of pleasure rather than a lover of God? Comment on how this is related to giving in to various forms of temptation.

6. Today, continually ask yourself if you are a lover of pleasure or a lover of God. Write down any times this thought helps you to overcome temptation.

7. This passage talks about people who have a form of godliness, but deny its power. Reflect on your memory verse. How could you better tap into the power of God in overcoming temptation?

For those of us with a weight control problem, temptations will be daily, but God provides mercy and grace to help us in our time of need so that we will not succumb. We need only approach His throne of grace.

DAY 4 . . . .
Record your Food Journal and Habit Graph.

Read Deuteronomy 8:10-14.
8. What are we instructed to do after we have eaten and are satisfied? Why do you think that is? What are we instructed not to do?

9. What relationship is there between thankfulness and eating slowly and enjoying your food?

DAY 5 . . . .
Record your Food Journal and Habit Graph.

Read 1 Corinthians 10:12-13.
10. What danger is mentioned here? What applications are there for you in a weight control program?

11. What promises has God made to us in regard to our temptations? Give some examples of this in regard to food temptation.

12. Is it a sin to be tempted? Explain.

As sinners, we all have an inclination toward sin. One individual may have a bent toward homosexuality, another toward drunkenness, another toward lying, and another toward gluttony, but God has stated that all of these are sin. So, regardless of our inclination, God has called us to be obedient, and He has equipped us with the resources to do so.

DAYS 6 AND 7 . . . .
Record your food plan and Habit Graph. Keep using the Word of God to overcome temptation! Read and complete the nutrition section.

NUTRITION PRINCIPLE

The importance of exercise. Exercise is one of the most critical factors for long-term success in weight control. Aerobic or endurance exercise (walking, jogging, biking, swimming, etc.) burns calories, providing a cushion for days when food intake may have exceeded body needs.

Several research projects have revealed that overweight people often don't eat more than other people (some of the research shows they eat less), but they do not burn off as many calories in the course of their daily activities. The overweight watch more TV, and are less active in their leisure time.

Exercise also tones muscle. Some exercise (such as weightlifting) increases muscle mass, which boosts metabolic rate. When muscles are toned, they take up less space, contributing to a loss of inches and a leaner look.

The discipline of being involved in an exercise program carries over into a lifestyle of discipline. When a woman is exercising, she is more likely to be disciplined in her eating habits. This leads to a feeling of well-being and bolstered self-esteem, which will make her desire to continue taking good care of herself.

Many overweight people don't get involved in exercise because they are uncomfortable about the way they look while exercising, or they don't know how to get started. If that is the case, the best way to start is to contact a fitness club, an exercise physiologist, or a wellness program at your local hospital or place of business, and get guidance. If you're over 35 years of age, have never exercised before, or are extremely overweight, it would be wise to also get a physical and your doctor's input before beginning an exercise program.

The best exercises for burning calories and improving your heart health are ones that are continuous, keeping your heart rate up. Some of them are listed below. Look through them, and determine what you would enjoy, what you can afford, and what is available to you, considering the weather and the facilities in your community.

If you can find a friend who will exercise with you, all the better, because you can keep each other accountable when your motivation wanes.

brisk walking	jogging
running	biking
cross-country skiing	swimming
rowing	dancing
step aerobics	aerobic dance

True/False Test #4

1. T F   Research shows that many overweight people don't eat more, but they are less active and exercise less than lean people.
2. T F   Some of the best ways to tone muscle, burn calories, and increase a feeling of well-being are doing crossword puzzles, watching TV, and eating chips.

(See Appendix for answers.)

Application

This week I am going to overcome temptation by:

This week I am going to incorporate exercise into my life by:

Eight
The Power of Prayer

ACCOUNTABILITY TIME
Weigh in and record your progress on the graph in the Appendix.

As you are waiting to weigh in, or as you assemble afterward, share with a partner or small group:
A. Your memory verse (James 5:16).
B. Your Weight Graph, Habit Graph, and Food Journal.

WARMUP
Briefly share an exciting answer to prayer in your life — preferably a recent answer.

SPIRITUAL PRINCIPLE
The prayers of a righteous woman are powerful and effective.

DAY 1
Record your food plan and Habit Graph. Confess any sin in your eating habits, and turn from it. For example:

> I made chocolate chip cookies for the church youth group. The primary motive was to indulge myself. I could have provided ice cream and root beer for floats instead and I wouldn't have fallen. Next time, I must make no provision for the flesh.

53

1. Record your confessions about sinful eating habits below. As you pray for wisdom, record any thoughts God impresses on your heart.

Begin memorizing the following verse:

> Therefore confess your sins to each other and pray for each other so that you may be healed. The prayer of a righteous man is powerful and effective (James 5:16).

DAY 2
Record your food plan. Pray for the other group members by name, using Hebrews 12:11-13 for inspiration. Record your Habit Graph.

2. Ask God for wisdom concerning your eating habits. Then record any thoughts God impresses on your heart.

Finish memorizing James 5:16.

Read James 1:2-8.
3. Why should we consider it joy when we face trials in our weight control program? (vv. 2-4) Have you experienced the truth of this verse in your weight control program? Can you share a specific example?

4. How should we respond to trials or setbacks? (v. 5)

5. When we ask God for wisdom, what should our attitude be? Why? (vv. 6-8)

DAY 3

Record your food plan. Confess any sin in your eating habits, and turn from it. Record your Habit Graph.

6. What are some changes in your thinking or behavior for which you can thank God?

Read James 5:12-18.
7. What are some prerequisites for effective prayer listed in this passage?

Read Psalm 32:1-11.
8. What truths which you found in James concerning finding help from the Lord are also found in this psalm?

The Joy of Eating Right!

DAY 4

Record your food plan. Confess any sin in your eating habits and turn from it. Record your Habit Graph.

9. Record your confessions about sinful eating habits here. As you pray for wisdom, record any thoughts God impresses on your heart.

Read 1 Thessalonians 5:16-24.

10. What eight commands are we given in this passage? Which ones could you relate to weight control? How?

DAY 5

Record your food plan. Get out a hymnbook and sing at least two songs of praise to God. Record your Habit Graph.

Read Psalm 42:1-11.

11. What is one good response to discouragement, according to verses 5 and 11? How could you better make this a habit in your life?

Read Matthew 7:7-11.

12. What do the verbs *ask, seek,* and *knock* imply about effective prayer? Is there an application for your life?

13. What do you learn about God from this passage?

DAYS 6 AND 7

Record your food plan and Habit Graph. Keep asking God for wisdom and help! Read and complete the nutrition section.

NUTRITION PRINCIPLE

Lowering fat in meal preparation and cooking. Incorporate some of the following tips in your food preparation to reduce your fat and calorie intake.

Meats
    Buy leaner cuts.
    Trim all fat, remove poultry skin.
    Buy ground turkey instead of ground beef.
    Broil and throw away the fat.
    Fry with nonstick skillets and sprays.

Sauces
    Chill soups and stews to make the fat rise, then skim it off or use a fat-separating cup.
    Use diet margarine or a butter substitute.
    Use plain nonfat yogurt in place of sour cream or mayonnaise.
    Use fat free salad dressings and mayonnaise.
    Replace cream cheese with Neufchâtel cheese or fat free cream cheese.

In baking and cooking:
    Use zero calorie salad oil (recipe in Appendix) in place of oil in salad dressing recipes.
    Use half the amount of cream soup in casserole recipes and add skim milk in its place.
    Steam vegetables (don't sauté in butter!).
    Replace egg with two egg whites.
    Use nonfat dry milk in cooking.
    Use evaporated skim milk instead of cream.

Modify two of your favorite recipes to reduce their fat content and write them out below:

1.   2.

Application

One truth I've learned about prayer or through prayer which I will apply to my weight control program is:

When I go to the grocery store this week, I am going to plan to lower my fat intake by:

When I cook this week, I am going to lower my fat intake by:

Nine

Convictions

ACCOUNTABILITY TIME
Weigh in. Record your progress on the graph in the Appendix.

As you are waiting to weigh in, or as you assemble afterward, share with a partner or small group:
A. Your memory verse (Daniel 1:8).
B. Your Weight Graph, Habit Graph, and Food Journal.

WARMUP
Think of an area of your life where you hold a conviction. What is it? How did you come to feel so strongly about this?

SPIRITUAL PRINCIPLE
Defeated individuals have beliefs; successful ones have convictions.

DAY 1 . . . .
Record your food plan and Habit Graph.

Begin memorizing the following verse:

> But Daniel resolved not to defile himself with the royal food and wine, and he asked the chief official for permission not to defile himself this way (Daniel 1:8).

DAY 2 ·

Record your Food Journal and Habit Graph. Finish memorizing
Daniel 1:8.

1. Look up *conviction* in the dictionary. What are some synonyms?
   How does *conviction* differ from *belief?*

2. Read the following passages and determine what convictions
   the following individuals held. How did their convictions specifically impact their lives?

   A. Abraham (Romans 4:18-22)

   B. Paul (2 Timothy 1:12)

   C. Daniel (Daniel 1)

Daniel and his friends ate only vegetables for 10 days, because that
was the only healthy food available. Some have gone on the Daniel
diet and eaten only vegetables, but you could wisely add grains,
fruit, and limited low fat protein and milk.

DAY 3 ·

Record your Food Journal and Habit Graph. Review Daniel 1:8.

Read Luke 14:25-35.
3. What did Jesus tell the large crowds who were following Him?
   What do you think His purpose was?

4. What value is there in considering the cost for establishing convictions?

Dee's Reflection

When my sister Sally led me to Christ, I was a young wife and mother. First, she encouraged me to count the cost—telling me that I must be willing to go wherever God wanted me to go and to do, daily, whatever He wanted me to do. She suspected that He'd have me relinquish my dream of building an extravagant house overlooking the Pacific Ocean. (At the time, that seemed like an enormous sacrifice!) Because she encouraged me to count the cost, when I did surrender, it was with a strong sense of commitment. I've always been thankful to Sally for making me count the cost.

5. What are the costs involved in a lifelong weight control program? (What things will you have to give up, either temporarily or permanently?)

Peg's Reflection

As a "weight control disciple," I have experienced a cost. It takes time to exercise, to plan menus, to cook healthy recipes. It takes discipline to give up high-fat and high-calorie foods. The rewards, however, of knowing I am being obedient to Christ and having a healthy lean body, make it all worthwhile.

DAY 4
Record your Food Journal and Habit Graph.

6. According to Matthew 6:25-34, what should (*or shouldn't*) be our priorities in life?

The Joy of Eating Right!

Read Exodus 16:1-3.

7. Describe the attitude of the Israelites after they had been delivered out of slavery.

8. What would you describe as their priorities in life? Contrast their beliefs with Daniel's convictions.

DAY 5 ....

Record your Food Journal and Habit Graph.

9. Describe your feelings about each of the following, then determine whether these are beliefs or convictions.

Planning your menu for the day

Avoiding high-fat foods

Exercise

Becoming victorious in your eating habits

DAYS 6 AND 7 ....

Record your food plan and Habit Graph. Read and complete nutrition section.

NUTRITION PRINCIPLE

Lowering sugar and salt content in food preparation. Recipes for sweets can usually be altered to include less sugar. Check out the following suggestions:

1. Cut back on sugar in recipes by one fourth. If acceptable, try cutting back more next time.
2. Use sugar-free gelatin, sugar-free pudding, or sugar-free drink mixes in recipes.
3. Use juice pack or water pack fruits in recipes instead of those packed with heavy syrup.
4. Enhance sweetness by lightly adding "sweet spices," such as allspice, cardamon, cinnamon, ginger, nutmeg, cloves, and vanilla.
5. Purchase "Sweet Inspirations," a sugar-free dessert cookbook endorsed by the American Diabetes Association. (Cost including shipping and handling: $15.20) Write:
   > Sweet Inspirations
   > Imaginationary Books, Inc.
   > 1420 N.W. Gilman Blvd., Suite 2258
   > Issaquah, Washington 98027

The only recipes that will fail without salt are yeast breads and pickled salt brine solutions. You can omit salt in other recipes and also lower sodium content by:

1. Cooking frozen and fresh vegetables instead of canned.
2. Not adding salt when canning and freezing vegetables.
3. Don't add salt to cooking noodles, rice, hot cereal, or potatoes.
4. Replace garlic salt and onion salt with garlic powder and onion powder, using about one fourth the quantity.
5. Minimize the use of bouillon, canned soups, and packaged dinners in cooking.

True/False Test #5

1. T F Many recipes can have sugar reduced and sweetness enhanced with spices with little change in taste.
2. T F Canned vegetables are better for you than fresh or frozen vegetables.

(See Appendix for answers.)

Application

These are my convictions concerning weight control:

This week I am going to reduce sugar and salt in my diet by:

Ten

Perseverance

ACCOUNTABILITY TIME
Weigh in. Record your progress on the graph in the Appendix.

As you are waiting to weigh in, or as you assemble afterward, share with a partner or small group:
A. Your memory verse (Galatians 6:9).
B. Your Weight Graph, Habit Graph, and Food Journal.

WARMUP
Think about an area where you have persevered and seen fruit (raising obedient children, decorating your home, saving money, gardening, learning to play an instrument, etc.). What were some of the feelings you had along the way? And how did you feel when you saw fruit?

SPIRITUAL PRINCIPLE
If you don't give up sowing to the Spirit, you will be successful. You can begin your program with great motivation and perspective, but perseverance is necessary for lifelong success.

DAY 1 . . . .
Record your food plan. Record your Habit Graph.

Begin memorizing the following verse:

Let us not become weary in doing good, for at the proper time we will reap a harvest if we do not give up (Galatians 6:9).

DAY 2 . . . .

Record your Food Journal and Habit Graph. Finish memorizing Galatians 6:9.

Read Hebrews 12:1.
1. This verse refers to "the cloud of witnesses" which were described in Hebrews 11. These were heroes who persevered because of faith. What do you learn about them in each of the following passages, and how might you walk in their steps in your weight control program?

   A. Abraham (Hebrews 11:8-10, 17-19)

   B. Moses (Hebrews 11:24-27)

   C. Joshua (Hebrews 11:30)

2. What commands are given in Hebrews 12:1? Thoughtfully ask the Lord how this would apply to your weight control program, and write down what He impresses on your heart.

DAY 3 . . . .

Record your Food Journal and Habit Graph.

66

Read Hebrews 12:1-13.
3. Using a dictionary, define *perseverance*.

4. Who is the ultimate example of perseverance? How did He do it? (v. 2)

5. Twice the author of Hebrews exhorts us not to "lose heart." What motivation does he give?

6. How has the Lord disciplined you through the consequences of your disobedience? What would be a negative and a positive way to respond to that discipline?

7. Review your past memory verse of Hebrews 12:11. Share your reflections on this after having been through this 10-week program.

DAY 4
Record your Food Journal and Habit Graph.

Read Galatians 6:7-9.
8. What natural consequence has God built into life? (vv. 7-8)

9. Give examples of how people have tried to escape this natural consequence in weight control and have deceived themselves. Have you done this? Explain. (Consider the habits from the Habit Graph. For example, what happens if you skip planning your meals?)

10. Give consequences of the following examples of sowing to the flesh.

   A. Action: Consequences?
      Eating one potato chip

   B. Action: Consequences?
      Purchasing chocolate donuts

   C. Action: Consequences?
      Other

11. Give consequences of the following two examples of sowing to the Spirit.

   A. Action: Consequences?
      Prayerfully planning meals
      and snacks for the day

B. Action: Consequences?
   Meeting a friend to walk
   and pray with each day

C. Action: Consequences?
   Other

DAY 5 . . . .
Record your food plan honestly. Don't deceive yourself! Record
your Habit Graph. Be honest!

Review Galatians 6:9.
12. What promise is given in this verse? What is the condition of
    the promise?

13. Have you seen this promise fulfilled in other areas of your
    life?

14. What causes you to become discouraged in your weight con-
    trol program and to want to give up? What do you think could
    help you overcome the desire to give up?

We began this study with the need for group support. It's interest-
ing that Paul's admonition to persevere is in the same context as
supporting one another (Galatians 6:1-2). You may want to consid-

er how to continue supporting one another in your small group. Here are some suggestions for perseverance. Read them over prayerfully.

It would be unrealistic to expect to change a lifetime of poor eating habits in 10 weeks. You have begun to change, but it's vital to plan to persevere with the support of a friend or friends who will hold you accountable — for at least another 10 weeks. Here are some ways to persevere:

1. Do this study again, right away.
2. Do another study in this series (see the back cover), but continue with the disciplines of the Food Journal, Habit Graph, and Weight Graph. Begin your session with weighing in and pairing off for accountability for these three disciplines each week. My books, *The Friendships of Women* and *The Lifestyles of Christian Women* (Victor) with accompanying leader's guides, could be used for study.
3. Choose a book from the recommended reading list and read a little each day. Meet with a friend weekly and be accountable for a Food Journal, Habit Graph, and Weight Graph. We would especially recommend *Love Hunger* (Thomas Nelson, 1990), which has an accompanying workbook.

15. What direction would you like to see your small group take?

DAYS 6 AND 7 . . . .

Record your food plan and Habit Graph. Read and complete the nutrition section.

NUTRITION PRINCIPLE

Learning the importance of planning when eating away from home.
Americans eat one out of every three meals away from home, and

they tend to overeat when they eat out. Having a game plan is crucial. Read this over before you go out, and plan your strategy!

Whenever possible, pack your lunch!
1. You're stronger in the morning—and you're more likely to choose your menu and portion size wisely, avoiding the hidden fat and calories of restaurant food.
2. Don't get in a rut. A "brown bag" lunch does not have to be a sandwich, chips, cookies, and fruit. Refrigeration and a microwave add options. Consider some of the following:

Chef's salad	Low-fat yogurt
Cottage cheese	Bagels, muffins, breads
Soups, stews	Leftovers (planned overs)

When you'll be eating in restaurants, consider the type of restaurant you'd prefer and don't be passive in expressing your preference.

FAST-FOOD RESTAURANTS
1. Get as much information as possible on the calorie and fat content of the menu items. Most chains have these available.
2. Be careful of salad bars. If you have a tendency to load up on the higher calorie items, then a sandwich might be a lower calorie option.

CAFETERIA/BUFFETS
1. Avoid "all you can eat" buffets until you've been in control for over a year.
2. Look over the selections available to you before you begin to make your choices.
3. Take only one plate for your salad and entree and set a "two inch" rule. You will not pile your plate higher than two inches.
4. Split a dessert with someone, or just have a bite of another's dessert.

ORDER OFF THE MENU RESTAURANTS
1. Be assertive. Don't be afraid to ask how dishes are prepared or to ask the waitress to modify to suit your needs.

2. Ask for dressings and toppings such as butter and sour cream to be served on the side.
3. Ask for chicken, fish, or other items to be broiled or grilled rather than fried.
4. Ask for sauces or gravies to be left off of meats and vegetables.
5. Have the waitress serve the bread with the meal, rather than before.
6. Ask for low calorie dressings, fresh fruits, and plain items, even if they're not on the menu.
7. Order an appetizer in place of an entree, but ask that it be served with the entrees.
8. When your meal arrives, if the portion size is too large, ask for a doggie bag right away, cut off what you don't plan to eat, and put it away immediately.
9. Leave a generous tip if you've made several requests—and a hearty thank you!

EATING AT ANOTHER'S HOME
1. If you know you can't handle the social pressure, it may be better to refuse an invitation than to overeat.
2. When invited out, let the hostess know she doesn't need to make dessert or lavish dishes for you.
3. Offer to bring something, so you know there will be at least one low-calorie option.
4. Eat slowly. You'll avoid seconds, but be assertive about refusing seconds and large amounts. Be appreciative of cooperation.
5. If possible, remove your plate when you are done. This is a public commitment that you're through eating.

Application
What plan could you have for the following situations?

1. You can't go home from work for lunch. The office has a refrigerator and a microwave—or, you can eat out.

2. You're going to a fast-food restaurant with a friend for supper.

3. Your adult Sunday School class is having a potluck.

4. What is your plan for persevering with your weight control program?

Leader's Helps

BEFORE THE FIRST SESSION

This study will differ from the other studies in this series in that each week will begin with an Accountability Time. To prepare for that, you will need to:

1. Find a place to meet where a balance scale is available. Make sure privacy is possible, perhaps by having the scale in a separate room so that the members can wait outside in line.

2. Locate the Leader's Chart of Members' Actual Weights in the Appendix. Each week record the members' actual weights and keep them confidential. They will also need to record their weight loss or gain on their individual charts. This chart does not show actual weight, though they may opt to record it.

3. Make participants aware of the commitment factor in this study. Many who have never been interested in Bible study before will be interested in this study. However, weight control support groups have a high drop-out rate, so let them know ahead of time that they should not sign up unless they are committed to coming every week for 10 weeks and doing the disciplines of Bible study, the Food Journal, and the Habit Graph. Jesus asked people to count the cost before they followed Him, and it is legitimate to do so now. Let them know you are limiting enrollment so they should not sign up unless committed. The group should be no larger than 15.

4. Have at least one copy of *The Can Have Diet Book* (see Appendix for ordering information) on hand. Although there is a choice of food plans, most people prefer more direction. This plan offers great flexibility and will enable them to count their fat intake, which recent research shows is vital. Women who

are eating 1,200 calories a day but 50% fat may not lose weight, whereas women who are eating 1,200 calories a day with 20% fat are likely to lose weight.

ACCOUNTABILITY TIME

Each week group members will weigh in and also share with a partner: their memory work, Food Journal, and Habit Graph. This could be done in line as they arrive, if they develop the habit of pairing with the next available woman in line. Or, if time permits, you can do this when you reassemble in your circle.

THE DISCUSSION

Your role is key! It's vital to remember that the real teacher is the Holy Spirit and you must not get in His way. People remember best what they discover and articulate themselves, rather than what they are taught. To help them do this, keep these guidelines in mind:

1. Think of yourself as a discussion leader rather than a teacher. Ask the questions and allow silences until the Spirit prompts an answer from a group member—most of the time you will not be answering the questions yourself. If group members ask a question, throw it back to the group.
2. Direct the group members to look in the Scripture for their answers. For example, ask: "What does Luke 10:40 say about this?"
3. Place chairs in as small a circle as possible. Space inhibits sharing.
4. Draw out shyer members by occasionally going around the room, giving people the freedom to pass. Once you get to know your shyer members, you may feel led to ask them what they think if their facial expression indicates readiness.
5. If you have a monopolizer, take action or your group may be destroyed:

Pray for wisdom for yourself and for control on the part of the monopolizer.

Try to sit next to rather than opposite her. Looking at her often prompts her to talk.

Ask: "What does someone else think?" "Can we hear from someone else?"

Find ways to meet her emotional needs, which is often the root cause for her excess talking. Draw her out before the discussion begins about her life. Encourage her beforehand as well (about her appearance, her punctuality, even her control, if she has shown some, in the discussion time).

If the problem persists, *it is your responsibility* as a leader to talk to her privately. Here's one approach: "Ellie — I've been concerned about how little the shyer members talk. I love to talk and I know you do too — and you have lots of good things to share. But because we jump in so quickly, or share for too long, the shyer members don't have time to reflect or respond. I think if we would each occasionally ask, 'What do some of the rest of you think?' we'd have more sharing."

6. Keep the discussion on track. Some gentle women leaders lose control of discussions. You don't want this study to turn into a coffee klatsch, so balance freedom with moving gently through the study. If you are having trouble completing the lessons in your allotted time, circle the optional questions (which will be listed in the following chapter helps) and skip them in discussion.

7. If a beginner gives a wrong answer, let it go unless it's a matter of salvation. Simply ask, "What does someone else think?" The Holy Spirit will generally prompt someone besides you to give a right answer. A direct correction from the leader may hurt the group member badly enough to drop out. Expect them to do their action assignments and memory work. Don't dodge the questions asking them to share on these things. And be a good example, being willing to go first. If they are sluggish, call a friend or two from the group and ask them to be a good example with you.

PRAYER TIME

Women's emotional and spiritual needs are met during the prayer time. Ideally, your group should meet for two hours (30 minutes for weighing in and accountability, 60 minutes for discussion, and 30 minutes for prayer). A group often bonds because of a time of sharing requests and praying for one another, and this may help them stick out what is probably one of the most demanding studies they've ever experienced. If you have 30 minutes, you can minister to other concerns in addition to eating right.

Leader's Helps for Chapter 1
Support Groups

THE FIRST SESSION
Begin by sitting down around a table, or as in tight a circle as possible. Have group members turn to the Appendix and show them four items:

1. The choice of food plans, which they will need to decide upon before they begin this study. Show them *The "Can Have" Diet* book.
2. The Weight Graph which does not show actual weights, though they can list their weight if they want to; the leader's chart which does show actual weights but will be kept confidential by the group leader.
3. The Habit Graph in which they will record daily.
4. The food plan in which they will record what they plan to eat (and what they actually eat) in a separate notebook.

Explain that though this may seem overwhelming, only the Habit Graph and the food plan are daily disciplines. The only other discipline is their Scripture study which has been broken down into small daily sections.

Then ask group members to get in line so you can weigh them. Assure them that they will have privacy and that you will keep their weights confidential. Then return to your circle.

WARMUP
Have them share their name, a little about themselves, and why they've come to this group.

HELPS FOR SPECIFIC QUESTIONS
Question #3. If they need help, ask: **How did Jesus tap into the power of God?** (Prayer, including group prayer, knowing the Word, obedience.)

Question #4. One of the best ways to encourage one another daily is by being faithful in completing your own disciplines (the homework, the memory work, the Food Journal, the Habit Graph). Another is prayer.

Question #6. The hope we profess is that Christ, who died for our sins, is now alive and faithfully interceding for us, ready to give us His power.

Question #7. Be ready to lead the way, sharing how Christ has changed the way you spend your money, relate to your husband, raise your children, make entertainment choices, etc. Be specific concerning how He has helped you find victory in this area.

Question #8. After Question #9, there's a comment by Dee about our tendency to empathize with rather than gently confront sin. After discussing this comment, do a little role-playing. Ask a woman to respond to you in the wrong way, and another in the right way when you say: "I didn't do well this week. I didn't plan my eating or record it, or keep my Habit Graph."

Leader's Helps for Chapter 2

Perspective

ACCOUNTABILITY TIME

Weigh the group members. Record their weights on your chart and have them record their progress on their Weight Graphs. If you are short on time, they can pair off and be accountable to each other while they are waiting to be weighed. A responsible group member might help you with this, instructing the women to pair off as they arrive.

WARMUP

You may need to lead the way in sharing a stressful situation, modeling brevity and vulnerability.

HELPS FOR SPECIFIC QUESTIONS

Question #3. It's good to face the reality of pain for it will help you endure it. Take some time with this question.

Question #4. This is a key question. Talk about how thin people respond to pain or boredom, how fast they eat, what they do when they are full. Because these are not natural responses for most group members, *planning* is key. Talk about planning in your Food Journal as well as alternative responses to pain.

Question #7. This is a good balance to Question #3. Take some time here.

Question #9. Be sure you have answered this question carefully. You may need to share first to be a model.

Ask group members to share the main points in the nutrition section. Make sure they cover planning ahead, including planning deviations, and planning a balanced diet. Then ask if a few would be willing to share how they are doing with their Food Journals.

If time permits, have everyone share their answers to the application questions at the end. Have "Popcorn Prayer," particularly praying for perspective. If time permits, take other requests. Assign Chapter 3.

The Joy of Obedience

Part of your responsibility as a leader is to be a model. Paul said, in Philippians 4:9a, "Whatever you have learned or received or heard from me, *or seen in me* — put it into practice." Have your memory work word perfect. Plan and record your Food Journal thoroughly and honestly. Keep your Habit Graph honestly. Share any of these during discussion time as a model.

WARMUP
If group members are shy about sharing, you might call on a few individually. Perhaps you know they had a weight loss, or perhaps they shared something positive with you about their habits.

HELPS FOR SPECIFIC QUESTIONS
Question #2. Romans 12:2 talks about "renewing our minds." This would be an opportunity to stress the value of memory work. Even if they can't retain it a year from now, right now it is renewing their minds, strengthening them to make right choices.

Question #4. "Living" means that obedience must be an ongoing decision. Daily we must keep our Food Journals, make wise choices, confess our sins, and get back on track.

Question #7. You may need to provide a model for sharing specifically and vulnerably. For example, "Two nights ago I nibbled away at a pie until I'd eaten a third of it. I went to bed feeling very depressed. I know that if I'd resisted, I would have felt good about myself the next day."

Question #8. Again, you may need to lead the way.

Questions #9, #10, and #11. After answering these questions, go around the room and ask each woman to share one thing she learned about herself from these "reflective" questions, giving each the freedom to pass.

Take time to share responses to the application questions and then pair off for prayer or have "Popcorn Prayer." Assign Chapter 4. Warn group members that they will be sharing their Food Journals and Habit Graphs and memory work with the whole group next time.

Leader's Helps for Chapter 4
Self-Control

ACCOUNTABILITY TIME
Ask each person to share *one* of the four items where she has had some victory (memory work, Habit Graph, Food Journal, or Weight Graph) and make a comment on it.

WARMUP
This question is designed to help group members see that vows really can strengthen a person's self-control. However, those vows are weakened if the person has no fear of God.

HELPS FOR SPECIFIC QUESTIONS
Question #2. Some reasons are found in #4b and #6b.

Question #3. Sin quenches the Spirit, and, as this passage says, we all have sin at work within us. To be released, we must confess our sins, and then, with real repentance, turn from them, and Jesus Christ will cleanse us and empower us. If they need help, refer them to 1 John 1:9–2:2.

Question #4. The natural response would be to indulge the flesh. The reflective response would be to listen to the Spirit. Slowing down and asking questions about what you really want can help. It's also important to flee temptation—you might ask them for suggestions on what to do with the chocolate chip cookies that are calling to you.

Question #5. Discuss the following insights.
vv. 1-4: Again, they should discover that Jesus, through His death on the Cross, has the power to cleanse us from sin. You might wish to talk about the importance of keeping short accounts. How quickly and sincerely do they ask for forgiveness when they go off their food plan?

vv. 5-8: Take some time with this crucial passage. Ask them for specific applications for verse 5. Use verse 7 to talk about submitting to God when planning food choices, when shopping, when eating out.

vv. 13-14: Make sure they understand that the power for "putting to death" the sins of the flesh comes not from themselves, but from the Spirit. We are to continually put our trust in Him.

Question #7. Honesty and faithfulness in recording will make both of these more effective tools.

If time permits, ask them to help you make a list of "Food Friends" and "Food Enemies" based on this week's and last week's nutrition sections. Explain that while no food is evil (Peter's experience in Acts 10 exemplifies this) still, if we overindulge in foods that are high in fat, cholesterol, salt, or sugar, we will harm our bodies. First Corinthians 6:12 says: " 'Everything is permissible for me' — but not everything is beneficial. 'Everything is permissible for me' — but I will not be mastered by anything." Ask them what foods hurt them when they overindulge? What foods tend to master them?

Ask them to share the answers to their application questions and then have "Popcorn Prayer" for one another. Assign Chapter 5.

BEFORE YOU MEET AGAIN
Call or write every group member, encouraging her to persist in attendance and letting her know that you are going to begin next week by affirming each other.

The Heart

WARMUP

Affirming one another will bond your group, so this is an important exercise. This study is difficult in its high standards, so bonding will help encourage attendance! If you feel certain everyone understands the plan of salvation, you can spend more time on this. But if not, you would be wise to divide a large group and to limit to four the number of times a woman can be affirmed.

HELPS FOR SPECIFIC QUESTIONS

Question #2. The heart in Scripture means "the innermost center" of man, including his mind, his feelings, his moral character.

Question #3. If you are behind schedule, you may want to skip this question and come back to it so that you will be sure to cover the plan of salvation.

Question #5. You might want to make tracts available, such as Campus Crusade's *The Four Spiritual Laws* (available in Christian bookstores). You could also explain the plan of salvation on a poster board with a diagram showing the great gulf between man and God, how Christ bridged it on the Cross, and how we must put our trust in that salvation. Ask a few volunteers to share their sentences without elaboration.

Question #9. She is saving 500 calories a day—3,500 divided by 500 is 7. So she will lose 1 pound in 7 days, or 10 pounds in 10 weeks.

Leader's Helps for Chapter 6
Appetite and Hunger

HELPS FOR SPECIFIC QUESTIONS

Question #1. You might ask group members to turn back to Genesis 4:6-7 to see that Cain gave Satan a foothold the first time he disobeyed God's instructions. Help them to see the danger of going off their food plan for the first time each day. Or the danger of putting the first "off the list" item in their grocery cart.

Question #4. Ask for specific suggestions for controlling oneself from "grazing" while preparing meals, or going on a binge with ice cream or chips.

Question #5. Explain that Ecclesiastes is a portrait of a man trying to find fulfillment outside of Christ. You might ask them if finding fulfillment in Christ is changing their attitude about food. What about other areas of appetite such as money or sex?

Questions #12 and #13. You might want to go around with these questions, asking women to respond to one or both of them briefly, giving them the freedom to pass.

Ask them to share the answers to their application questions and then have Popcorn Prayer for one another. Assign Chapter 7.

Overcoming Temptation

WARMUP
It would be best if group members could come up with their own Scriptures. However, if you have a group of beginners who are very unfamiliar with Scripture, you might have them turn to Philippians 4:4-13 and choose a passage that could help them overcome the temptation to watch, or do, or say something displeasing to God.

HELPS FOR SPECIFIC QUESTIONS
Question #3. Jesus would have given Satan a foothold. Jesus never did that because He kept His eyes set on the joy before Him.

Question #4. Take some time with this question, hearing from many. Possible Scriptures might include:

    A. Romans 13:4; Ephesians 4:27
    B. 1 Corinthians 10:13; Matthew 11:28
    C. Proverbs 20:4; Galatians 6:9

Question #9. Studies show that thin people are more aware of what they eat as they are eating. Being thankful, as you are eating, can make you savor every bite and be more satisfied when you are done.

Question #11. Often the way of escape is literally, turning and running. Sometimes that is not possible, and we must stand up under it. Then, the way of escape is our thought life. Ask members to give examples of right thinking when they cannot flee and must stand up to temptation.

Ask them to share the answers to their application questions and then have Popcorn Prayer for one another. Assign Chapter 8.

Leader's Helps for Chapter 8
The Power of Prayer

You may want to look at suggestions for followup (at the end of Chapter 10). You will need to order guides or books for your group now in order for them to arrive on time.

HELPS FOR SPECIFIC QUESTIONS

Question #1. You may need to start modeling vulnerability.

Question #3. If they need help coming up with an example of how the testing of their faith develops perseverance, stimulate their thinking by asking: **Do any of you feel you've gotten stronger as you've been obedient in this weight control program? Is it easier to persevere in the evening with weight control if you've been obedient during the day?**

Question #8. In particular they should find the importance of confessing sin (James 5:16; Psalm 32:5) and asking for wisdom (James 1:5; Psalm 32:9).

Question #10. Be joyful always (don't grumble about temporary pain); Pray continually (in food planning, in grocery shopping, in eating out); Give thanks in all (for discipline, for forgiveness); Don't put out the Spirit's fire (be sensitive to His leading); Don't treat prophecies with contempt (obey the Word); Test everything (appetite or hunger?); Hold onto the good (healthy food, complex carbohydrates, low fat); Avoid every kind of evil (gluttony!).

Bring out your low-fat cooking tools and ask if any have used one or more and liked them. Give them an opportunity to look at each other's recipes and possibly exchange them. Share answers to application questions. Pair off for prayer, asking them to confess their sins to one another, and to pray for wisdom and strength in their weight control program. Assign Chapter 9.

Leader's Helps for Chapter 9
Convictions

WARMUP
This could easily turn into a long discussion since people like to talk about, even argue, convictions. You may need to step in, as the purpose of this Warmup is simply to see the motivating strength of convictions. You don't want to cut into the study time.

HELPS FOR SPECIFIC QUESTIONS
Question #1. You could point out that James said the demons believe that there is one God and shudder (James 2:19). If you simply have beliefs about weight control, they may make you uncomfortable, but they don't change your behavior.

Question #2. Help them discover phrases like "fully persuaded" and "convinced" and "resolved," by asking: **What phrases in these passages demonstrate the idea of convictions?** You might also draw them out by asking how you think someone gets to the point of being fully persuaded.

Question #4. The Parable of the Sower seems to indicate that those who expected difficulties were the most likely to face them victoriously (Matthew 13:1-24).

Question #5. If the discussion seems negative, ask them what rewards there will be in exchange for the sacrifices.

Share answers to application questions. Have Popcorn Prayer or pair off for prayer, asking them to pray for one another, that they would trade their beliefs for convictions. Assign Chapter 10.

Perseverance

HELPS FOR SPECIFIC QUESTIONS
Question #2. You might want to hear from everyone on this question, giving the freedom to pass.

Question #6. Discipline can come in the form of consequences or conviction. A negative response would be to lose heart and give up. A positive response would be repentance and persistence.

Question #7. Encourage them to share some of their successes: weight loss, change in habits, peace.

Question #9. Eating disorders such as bulimia are examples of this deception. But for most of us, we deceive ourselves by failing to measure food or to count the handful of Cheerios we grab when putting away the box.

Question #10. In addition to the obvious consequences of depression—giving Satan a foothold and gaining weight—ask them to consider how disobedience in eating impacts obedience in other areas of their lives. You might also ask how it impacts their children or spouses.

Question #11. In addition to the obvious consequences of feeling good and losing weight, ask them to consider how obedience in eating impacts obedience in other areas of their lives. You might also ask how it impacts their children or spouses.

Question #13. If sharing is slow, ask: **Can you think of something you prayed about for a long time—and then finally, God answered? Or a ministry dream which you have seen come true? Or an area where you have seen growth in your**

life—such as controlling your tongue, studying the Bible, or listening to Christian radio?

Question #16. Read over the suggestions for perseverance. Also check out the list of recommended reading.

Stress that eating right is a lifestyle and that group members will need continuing group support. When their Habit Graphs have an average passing grade (7 points) for a month straight, they may no longer need weekly group support. However, it would be wise to have a prayer partner who will keep you accountable. It will get easier as your tastes, habits, and thinking change—but it will always take discipline.

True and False Answers

TEST #1
1. F
2. T
3. T

TEST #2
1. F
2. F
3. T

TEST #3
1. F
2. T
3. T

TEST #4
1. T
2. F

TEST #5
1. T
2. F

CHAPTER 5
Understanding calorie balance
9. 3,500 cal/pound x 10 pounds =
    35,000 cal ÷ 50 calories =

70 days

Sample Recipes

QUICK BEEF STROGANOFF
³/₄ lb. sirloin steak
8 oz. sliced fresh mushrooms
½ medium onion, sliced
1 clove garlic
10 ½ oz. can cream of mushroom soup
2 Tbsp. catsup
2 tsp. Worcestershire sauce
1 cup plain nonfat yogurt
8 oz. noodles, cooked

Brown steak, mushrooms, onion, and garlic over medium heat. Add mushroom soup, catsup, and Worcestershire sauce and heat thoroughly. Add yogurt and serve over cooked noodles.
   Yield: 4 servings 1 serving = 445 calories, 12 gm. fat

SUNSHINE CARROTS
5 medium carrots cut crosswise on bias
1 Tbsp. sugar
1 tsp. cornstarch
¼ tsp. ground ginger
¼ cup orange juice

Cook carrots in water until just tender (about 20 minutes). Combine all other ingredients in small saucepan and cook until thick. Pour over hot drained carrots and toss.
   Yield: 4 servings 1 serving = 55 calories, 0 gm. fat

DOUBLE CRISPY CHICKEN
3 ½ lb. chicken, cut up and skinned
1 cup skim milk
1 cup flour
1 tsp. pepper
1 cup cornflake crumbs
2 Tbsp. margarine

Mix milk, flour, and pepper together and dip chicken pieces in mixture. Roll in crushed cornflake crumbs. Place on nonstick cookie sheet. Drizzle with margarine. Bake at 350° for 1 hour.
  Yield: 6 servings   1 serving = 330 calories, 11 gm. fat

SPAGHETTI SALAD
1 lb. spaghetti, cooked
2 tomatoes, diced
2 cucumbers, diced
2 green peppers, diced
1 onion, diced
1 lb. shredded mozzarella cheese
16 oz. bottle of oil-free Italian dressing
1 bottle Salad Supreme (in the spice section)

Mix all ingredients together and refrigerate for several hours before serving.
  Yield: 16 servings   1 serving = 215 calories, 5 gm. fat

FAT-FREE RAISIN COOKIES
1 cup flour
1 cup quick oats
$\frac{1}{2}$ cup sugar
$\frac{1}{2}$ tsp. baking soda
$\frac{1}{2}$ tsp. cinnamon
2 egg whites
$\frac{1}{3}$ cup corn syrup
1 tsp. vanilla
$\frac{1}{2}$ cup raisins

Combine flour, oats, sugar, baking powder, baking soda, and cinnamon. Mix egg whites, corn syrup, and vanilla. Add to dry ingredients. Add raisins. Drop on sprayed cookie sheet and bake at 375° for 10 minutes.
  Yield: 3 dozen cookies   1 cookie = 45 calories, 0 gm. fat

FRUIT DIP

1 pkg. sugar-free vanilla instant pudding mix
1 cup skim milk
1 cup nonfat plain yogurt

Beat pudding mix, yogurt, and skim milk together with electric mixer until thick. Chill. Serve with fresh fruit.
    Yield: 2 cups   2 Tbsp. = 15 calories, 0 gm. fat

ZERO-FAT SALAD OIL

1 cup cold water
2 ½ tsp. cornstarch

Mix water and cornstarch together and cook over medium heat until thickened, stirring constantly. Cool. Use in place of vegetable oil in salad dressing or salad recipes.
    Yield: 1 cup   1 cup = 30 calories, 0 gm. fat

VEGETABLE DIP

1 tsp. instant minced onion
4 oz. light cream cheese (Neufchâtel cheese)
½ tsp. Worcestershire sauce
¼ tsp. dry mustard
¼ tsp. garlic powder
½ tsp. parsely flakes
½ cup plain nonfat yogurt

Combine onion and 1 Tbsp. water. Let stand 5 minutes. Combine softened cheese, Worcestershire sauce, mustard, garlic, and parsley. Add onion mixture. Fold in yogurt. Cover and chill.
    Yield: 1 cup   2 Tbsp. = 50 calories, 3 gm. fat

Recommended Reading List

General Nutrition Information

Dr. Jean Mayer's Diet and Nutrition Guide by Jean Mayer, Ph.D., and Jeanne P. Goldberg, Ph.D., R.D.: New York, Pharos Books, 1990.

The Tufts University Guide to Total Nutrition by Stanley Gershoff, Ph.D. and Catherine Whitney: New York, Harper and Row, New York, 1990.

Cookbooks

Better Homes and Gardens Low-Fat Meals: Des Moines, Iowa, Meredith Corporation, 1990.

Cooking Light Cookbook 1990: Birmingham, Alabama, Oxmoor House, 1990.

Microwave Diet Cookery: Low Calorie Menus for All Seasons by Marcia Cone and Thelma Snyder: New York, Simon and Schuster, 1988.

Weight Control

Diets Don't Work by Bob Schwartz, Ph.D., Houston, Texas, Breakthru Publishing, 1982.

Diets Still Don't Work by Bob Schwartz, Ph.D., Houston, Texas, Breakthru Publishing, 1990.

Habits, Not Diets: The Secret to Lifetime Weight Control by James M. Ferguson, M.D., Palo Alto, California, Bull Publishing, 1988.

Love Hunger by Dr. Frank Minirth, Dr. Paul Meier, Dr. Robert Hemfelt, and Dr. Sharon Sneed: Nashville, Tennessee, Thos. Nelson, 1989. (Recommended follow-up study)

Maximize Your Body Potential: 16 Weeks to a Lifetime of Effective Weight Management by Joyce D. Nash, Ph.D., 1986.

Straight Talk About Weight Control: Taking the Pounds Off and Keeping Them Off by Lynn Bennion, M.D., Edwin L. Biorman, M.D., James M. Ferguson, M.D., and the Editors of Consumer Reports Books, 1991.

Magazines

Cooking Light, to order write P.O. Box 830549, Birmingham,

Alabama 35282-9810. Bi-monthly.

Tufts University Diet and Nutrition Letter, to order write P.O. Box 57857, Boulder, Colorado 80322-7857.

Weight Watchers, to order call 1-800-525-0643. Monthly.

Diet Plans

Some women function best with great freedom in making selections; others do better when their plan is specifically prescribed. Below are several dietary programs that can provide you with a well-balanced diet as you learn the joy of eating right. Study these programs carefully and choose one that you feel will be effective for you. If you've had success with a well-balanced program in the past and it isn't included here, you may use it, but do make a firm commitment to it.

OPTION ONE
COUNTING CALORIES OR CALORIE POINTS

Use a calorie counting book or the calorie point system to keep track of calories. Calorie points are a simplified and flexible way to count calories. You probably can obtain a copy of it from an area dietitian (for a fee) or you can order it by contacting the following dietitian and ordering *The "Can Have" Diet* book. We recommend starting with this because it is simple, flexible, and will educate you about the calorie and fat content of foods.

> *The "Can Have" Diet and More: The Easy Guide to Informed Exercise and Food Choices* by Patricia M. Stein, R.D., M.S., M.A. and Norma J. Winn, R.D., M.S.
>
> Available from:
>
> N.C.E.S.
> P.O. Box 3018
> Olathe, KS 66062-8018
> Telephone orders: 1-800-445-5653

A 1,200 calorie diet is a sound weight control program for most women.

OPTION TWO
THE FOOD GROUP PLAN

Adhere to the following 1,200 calorie diet by eating the proper number of servings each day from each of the four basic food groups. This is well-balanced and eliminates the extra fats, sweets, and sauces that many people normally add.

Daily eat the following:
  2 servings of low-fat dairy products
  2 servings of lean meat or meat substitute
  4 servings of fruits and vegetables
  4 servings of grains—breads and cereals

Weekly you can include 2 servings of *other* items.

DAIRY PRODUCTS—Each of the following is considered a serving:
  1 cup of skim or 1% milk
  1 cup of nonfat or low-fat yogurt
  1 oz. of low-fat cheese

LEAN MEAT OR MEAT SUBSTITUTE—Each of the following is considered a serving:
  2 oz. cooked lean meat, fish, or poultry
  2 eggs
  2 oz. low-fat cheese
  ½ cup low-fat cottage cheese
  1 cup of dried peas or beans (pinto, navy, etc.)

FRUITS AND VEGETABLES—Each of the following is considered a serving:
  1 cup of raw diced fruit or vegetable
  ½ cup of fruit juice or vegetable juice
  ½ cup of cooked fruit
  ¾ cup of cooked vegetable

GRAINS, BREAD, AND CEREALS—Each of the following is considered a serving:

1 slice bread
1 oz. of cold cereal
$\frac{1}{2}$ cup of cooked cereal, rice, or grits
$\frac{1}{2}$ cup of cooked pasta
$\frac{1}{2}$ hamburger or hot dog bun
$\frac{1}{2}$ English muffin or bagel
6 saltine crackers

OTHER ITEMS — Each of the following is considered a serving:
2 Tbsp. of fat — butter, margarine, oils
1 piece of cake — 2x3 inch piece
2 cookies
1 small piece of any dessert
1 doughnut or sweet roll

OPTION THREE
COUNT FAT GRAMS

Keep your grams of fat intake to 20-30 grams per day. To do this effectively you will need to spend time reading labels and also purchase a resource book to give fat information on unlabeled items. Possible resources are *The Fat Counter* and *The Fat Attack Plan,* both by Annette B. Natow, Ph.D., R.D. and Jo-Ann Heslin, M.A., R.D. and published by Pocket Books, New York, 1990.

It is possible to keep your fat intake low, but still consume too many calories if you overeat sweets and starches, etc., so this program requires diligence and honesty to work.

OPTION FOUR
ELIMINATE FATS AND REDUCE SUGARS

This plan should be tried only after you have had a passing grade of 7 points on your Habit Graph for a month. Continue eating as in the past, but concentrate on eliminating fats and minimizing sweets in your diet. Consider what and when you eat and what it is that triggers an eating response. ALWAYS ask yourself: "Is this hunger? Do I really need to eat?" or "Is it appetite? Do I just want to eat?" If you can identify the two and learn to eat low calorie, nutritious foods to satisfy your hunger, and then to quit eating when your hunger is satisfied, you will be able to control your weight without counting calories or keeping track of servings.

The nutrition principle sections in the lessons will teach you about foods that are high in fat and sugar. These foods should be included on an occasional basis only in an effort to keep calorie intake low.

Food Journal Instructions

Date: Record the date.

Meal: Record B for breakfast, L for lunch, D for dinner, S for snack.

Planned Menu: Record what you plan to eat: preferably for a whole day, but at least before you eat!

Calories: Record the planned calories or fat grams or food group portions, depending which plan you are following.

Actual intake: Record what you really ate!

Calories: Record the actual calories or fat grams or food group portions of what you really ate.

Hungry? 0 for not at all, 1 for mildly, 2 for very, 3 for famished! This will help you realize the importance of learning to eat in response to hunger instead of food cues, emotional reasons, or the clock.

Menu Planner and Food Journal

DATE	MEAL	PLANNED MENU	FAT	ACTUAL INTAKE	FAT	HUNGRY?

Leader's Chart of Members' Actual Weights
(To be guarded with your life!)

Member	Wk 1	Wk 2	Wk 3	Wk 4	Wk 5	Wk 6	Wk 7	Wk 8	Wk 9	Wk 10
	185									

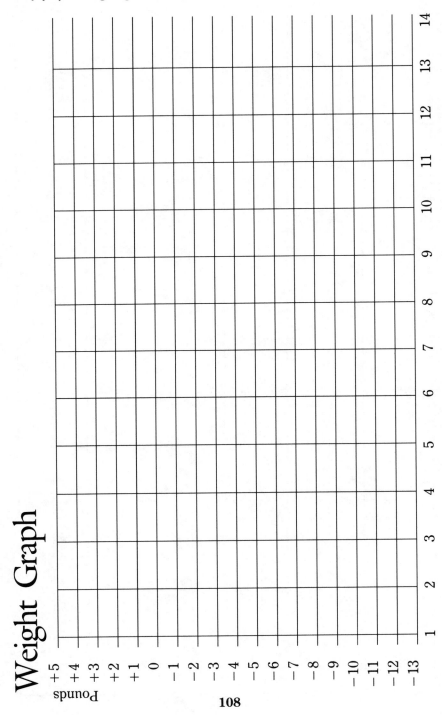

Weight Graph

Pounds

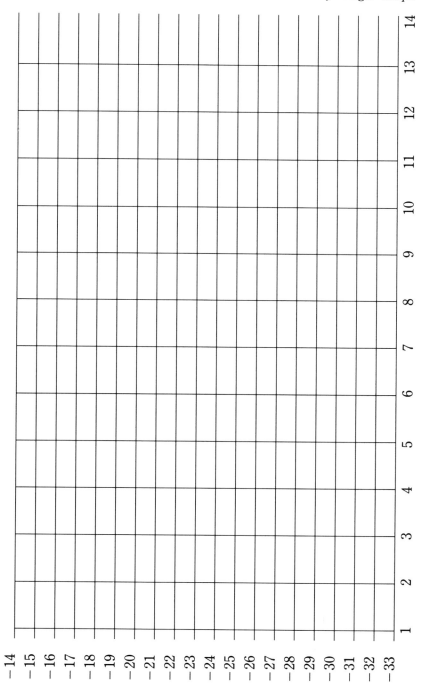

Habit Graph

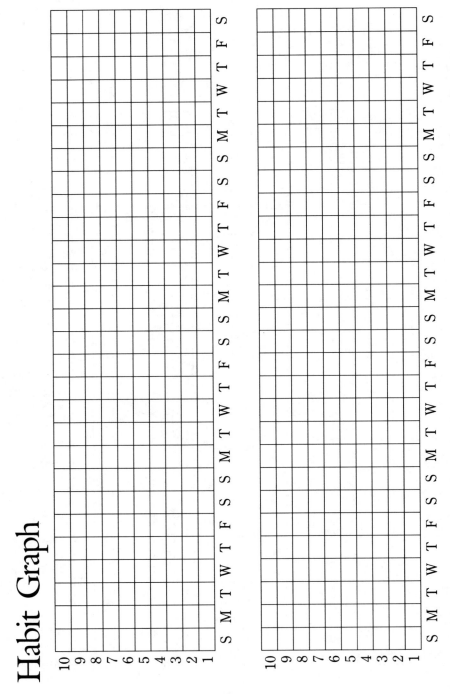

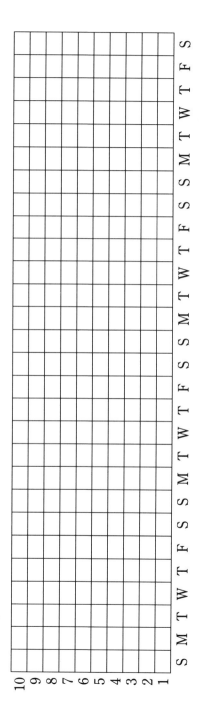

EVERY EVENING EVALUATE:

PLANNED	If you planned your day's menu:	2 points
FAT INTAKE	If you kept your fat intake low:	2 points
EXERCISED	If you exercised:	3 points
RECORDED	If you recorded *everything* you ate:	3 points